IRAQ
THEN AND NOW

John King

Produced for Raintree by
Monkey Puzzle Media Ltd.
Gissing's Farm, Fressingfield
Suffolk IP21 5SH, UK

First published in Great Britain by Raintree,
Halley Court, Jordan Hill, Oxford OX2 8EJ,
part of Harcourt Education.
Raintree is a registered trademark of Harcourt
Education Ltd.

Edited by Jenny Siklós and Paul Mason
Designed by Tim Mayer
Picture Research by Lynda Lines and Frances Bailey
Production by Duncan Gilbert
The consultant, Dr. Robert Stern, works as a part-time
analyst for the US State Department, primarily as part
of the War on Terror. He is a former Associate
Director for Counter-Terrorism.

Originated by Modern Age
Printed and bound in China by South China
Printing Company Ltd

ISBN 1 844 43205 X
10 09 08 07 06
10 9 8 7 6 5 4 3 2 1

British Library Cataloguing in Publication Data
King, John, 1939-
    Iraq then and now. - (The Middle East)
    1.Iraq - History - 1958- - Juvenile literature
    2.Iraq - Politics and government - 1958- - Juvenile
    literature
    I.Title
    956.7'043

Acknowledgements
The author and publisher are grateful to the
following for permission to reproduce copyright
material: AKG-Images p. **10** (Visioars); Camera
Press pp. **18**, **22** (Reza), **27** (Mohamed Ansar),
37 (Tina Paul); Corbis pp. **6** (Chris Ison/Reuters),
12 (Bettmann), **13** (Bettmann), **14** (Hulton-
Deutsch Collection), **23** (Ed Kashi), **26**, **30** (Les
Stone), **34** (Sean Adair/Reuters), **36** (Ray
Stubblebine/ Reuters), **43** (Ali Abu Shish), **47**
(Faleh Kheiber/Reuters); Empics pp. **3** (EPA), **33**
(EPA); Getty Images pp. **17** (Central Press), **19**
(AFP), **32** (Karim Sahib/AFP), **40** (Mauricio Lima),
46 (Wathiq Khuzaie); Popperfoto.com p. **15**;
Reuters pp. **4** (Steven Pearsall), **9** (Suhaib Salem),
39 (Zohra Bensemra), **45** (Thaier Al-Sudani); Rex
Features pp. **5** bottom (SIPA), **20** (SIPA), **21**
(SIPA), **24** (SIPA), **29** (SIPA), **35** (SIPA), **38**
(Eddie Mulholland/EMU), **41** (Lena Kara), **44**
(Ron Sachs/CNP); Topfoto pp. **16**, **25**, **28** (Roger
Viollet); Werner Forman Archive p. **7** (British
Museum, London).

Cover photograph shows Iraqi Shi'ite Muslims
throwing stones at the head of a broken statue of
Saddam Hussein in Sadr City, Baghdad, December
2003 (Getty Images/Ahmad Al-Rubaye).

Map illustrations by Encompass Graphics Ltd.

Every effort has been made to contact copyright
holders of any material reproduced in this book.
Any omissions will be rectified in subsequent
printings if notice is given to the publishers.

The paper used to print this book comes from
sustainable resources.

Contents

'We Got Him!' 4

The First Civilizations 6

Islam Comes to Iraq 8

Mongols, Kurds and Turks 10

1921: Britain Creates the Kingdom of Iraq 12

The Monarchy 1921–1958 14

Military Regimes 1958–1968 16

The Ba'ath in Power 1968–1979 18

Saddam as President 20

War with Iran 22

1990: The Invasion of Kuwait 24

1991: Iraq Driven Out of Kuwait 26

1991–2001: Sanctions and the Effects 28

1991–2002: The No-fly Zones 30

1991–2001: Sanctions and the Inspections 32

11 September: A Turning Point 34

Iraq and the United Nations 36

The Invasion of Iraq 38

Sunnis, Kurds and Shi'ites 40

2003–2004: Resistance Continues ... 42

Interim Government 44

Turbulent Iraq 46

Glossary 48

Facts and Figures 50

Timeline 51

Who's Who? 52

Find Out More 54

Index 55

Some words are shown in **bold**, like this. You can find out what they mean by looking in the Glossary.

'We Got Him!'

'We got him!' These were the words of Paul Bremer, the US Administrator in Iraq, who announced the capture of former Iraqi president Saddam Hussein, at a press conference on the afternoon of Sunday, 14 December 2003.

General Ricardo Sanchez, Commander of the US forces in Iraq (left), and Paul Bremer, announcing the capture of Saddam.

Since becoming the ruler of Iraq in 1979, Saddam Hussein had been cruel and brutal. He was captured in the town of al-Dawr, not far from Tikrit, on the evening of Saturday, 13 December 2003. Tikrit was Saddam Hussein's place of birth and had been the centre of his family's power. The former Iraqi **dictator**, who had once lived in a palace, was hiding in a concealed cellar near a farmer's shack. He had food, clothing and money, but was unshaven and confused. Though armed, he did not resist arrest.

The USA and its allies went to war against Saddam's Iraq in March 2003. Iraq was known to have had **chemical weapons**, and possibly also **biological weapons**, in 1991. It also had the beginnings of a nuclear weapons programme. In 2003 the USA and the UK believed action was necessary because they thought Saddam Hussein had been refusing to obey earlier **United Nations** resolutions. The resolutions demanded that he get rid of his **weapons of mass destruction**.

> **He was cowering in a hole in the ground. In the last analysis, he seemed not terribly brave.**
> (Donald Rumsfeld, US Secretary of Defence)

The invasion of Iraq began on 20 March with a major air attack on the Iraqi capital, Baghdad. At the same time, American and British troops moved into the south of the country, fighting their way north towards Baghdad. The invasion of Iraq was soon completed. American troops captured Baghdad on 9 April, and on 1 May, US President George W. Bush declared that the war was over. Though the USA hoped resistance would end with the capture of Saddam Hussein, this did not happen. Violence in Iraq continued. The puzzle was, how had Iraq's past led it to such a confrontation?

SADDAM'S WAR

Saddam Hussein defied the United Nations and the USA from the time of his invasion of Kuwait in 1991 up to 2003, when his regime was finally overthrown. United Nation sanctions had reduced Iraq to poverty. Iraq was allowed to sell oil for food, and 80 per cent of the population depended on this. But some of the money did not go to the ordinary Iraqis. Instead it went to Saddam and his associates. When the US-led invasion began, many Iraqis were relieved, hoping for an end to dictatorship and for a return of prosperity.

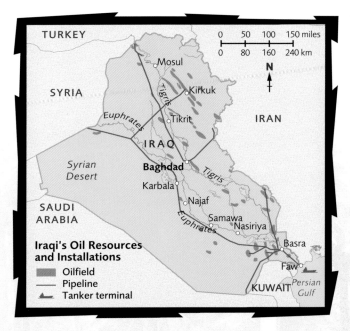

Iraqi's Oil Resources and Installations
- ▬ Oilfield
- — Pipeline
- ⚓ Tanker terminal

Iraq, its oil installations and its neighbours. Iraq's oil is crucial to the country's economy and the main reason for its importance in the Middle East.

US Marines taking up position on the outskirts of Baghdad, 7 April 2003.

The First Civilizations

Iraq lies in the ancient land known as **Mesopotamia**, which is the site of some of the earliest human settlements. Two great rivers, the Euphrates and Tigris, run through this land.

The culture of Sumer flourished in Mesopotamia 5,000 years ago, making it one of the world's oldest civilizations. The people of Sumer invented ways of **irrigating** their land, built brick houses and kept written records. They also began to study science, mathematics and astronomy.

Another achievement in early Mesopotamia was the writing of the first epic poems. The *Book of Gilgamesh*, dating from this time, tells the story of a legendary king who fought to preserve his city. Other poems were about the world's origins, and how the world was created by the gods.

> **" What a country can accomplish in the modern world is founded on its achievements in history. "**
> (Ra'id Abdul Ridha Mohammed, Iraqi archaeologist)

Iraqi fisherman on the Euphrates River. Traditional skills such as fishing have changed little since ancient times.

An ancient Sumerian wooden panel, made in around 2500 BCE, showing a banquet. The picture shows how the rulers of Sumer lived, 4,500 years ago.

Iraq is also the site of the city of Babylon, which is mentioned in the Bible, and is believed to have been built almost 4,000 years ago. Soon after, the region's King Hammurabi was the first to write down a system of laws. Later, about 2,500 years ago, another king, Nebuchadnezzar, built the Hanging Gardens of Babylon, one of the Seven Wonders of the Ancient World.

The land of Iraq next became part of the Empire of Persia, whose rulers lived to the east, in what is today Iran. In 331 BCE Alexander the Great conquered the country for the Greeks. Two hundred years later, the Persians recaptured Iraq. Persian rule continued until 636 CE, when Arab invaders arrived.

> **❝ Babylon was the capital of the world and the source of all the laws of humankind. ❞**
> (Saheb El-Doulaimy, a guide at the site of the ancient city)

ANCIENT TRADITIONS
'How many of us realize that if we fear bad luck when we see a black cat, or count time in 12 hours for each day and night or look up at the stars to read our fortune in the constellations, it was the civilization of ancient Iraq which invented all these things?'
(Leonard Woolley, archaeologist)

Islam Comes to Iraq

The Prophet Mohammed, the founder of the Muslim religion,
died in 632 CE. In the years after his death, the Arabs burst out
of Arabia and overran the lands known today as the Middle East,
including Iraq. Muslim Arabs first defeated the Persian rulers of
Iraq in 637 CE.

This key 637 CE battle between Persians and Muslim Arabs took place at
Qadisiyah, on the Euphrates River. This is near the modern Iraqi city of Najaf.
The Arabs defeated a Persian army led by an Iranian prince called Rustam.

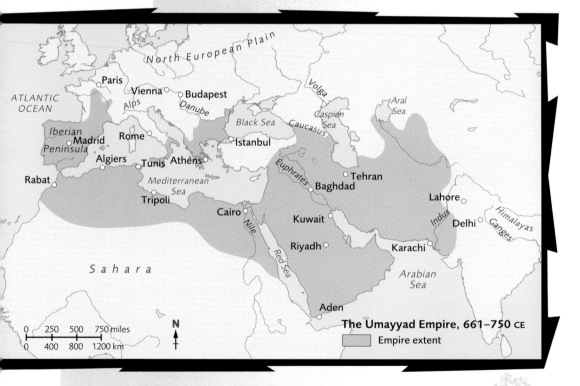

The Umayyad Empire, 661–750 CE
Empire extent

The Umayyads were a dynasty of Arabian Muslim Caliphs who ruled an empire stretching
from Spain to India. They came to power in 661 CE, following the death of the Prophet
Mohammed's cousin Ali (see page 9). In 750 CE they were overthrown by the Abbasids.

In 656 CE an argument over who should lead Islam broke out amongst the Muslims in Arabia. Ali, the Prophet Mohammed's cousin and son-in-law, believed he had the right to be leader, or **Caliph**, of the Muslims. Ali was recognised as Caliph in Iraq and Persia (modern Iran). But the Muslim rulers in Damascus chose another successor, Mu'awiya ibn Abi Sufyan. This led to a great division amongst Muslims, with the creation of two groups, the Shi'a, or **Shi'ite Muslims**, and the **Sunni Muslims**. The Shi'a, or the 'faction', followed Ali. The Sunni Muslims, who claimed they were following the customs laid down by Mohammed, backed Mu'awiya and the Caliphs who followed him.

In 661 CE Ali was murdered in the Iraqi city of Kufa, to the rage and despair of the Shi'a. In the coming centuries, the majority of Arabs would be Sunni Muslims, while the Shi'ite faith was mainly found amongst the Arabs of southern Iraq. Neighbouring non-Arab Iran also became almost entirely Shi'ite.

About 100 years later, the city of Baghdad was founded where the two great rivers, the Tigris and the Euphrates, meet. Baghdad became the capital of what is now Iraq. The region, and especially Baghdad itself, became the capital of the **Abbasid dynasty** and a great centre of Arabic culture, power and wealth.

The Abbasid Mosque at Samarra was built in 852 CE. When it was built, it was one of the largest mosques in the Islamic world.

THE SHI'ITE MUSLIMS

Today, there are many Shi'ites in southern Iraq, and they form 60 per cent of the country's total population. Neighbouring Iran is a Shi'ite country. Ali is buried in the Iraqi city of Najaf.

Mongols, Kurds and Turks

During the 13th century, Iraq was conquered by the Mongols, a tribal people from deep inside Asia. The Mongols swept westwards, mercilessly conquering and destroying all that lay in their path. Their chief, Hulagu, the grandson of Genghis Khan, seized Baghdad in 1258.

> **Again and again, almost the entire [population] of a city was massacred ... the terror was unprecedented.**
> *(Marshall C. Hodgson, a modern historian, describing the Mongol invasion)*

When the Mongols arrived, most Iraqis regarded themselves as Arabs and spoke Arabic. The separate culture of the **Kurds** had survived, however, along with other smaller cultural groups. Some Iraqis even continued to practise the Christian faith. These **minorities** are still present in 21st-century Iraq.

The Kurds, who lived in northern Iraq, also lived in neighbouring areas of Iran and Turkey. They spoke their own language, and regarded themselves as a separate people from the Arabs. They are mostly Sunni Muslims, though some are Shi'ites.

This illustration shows the siege of Baghdad by the Mongol army in 1258 CE. Hulagu, who led the army, warned the Caliph that he must surrender or his city and his land would be burned.

The Kurds are still culturally separate today, and many would like independence and their own country.

The Mongols were not Muslims, but soon converted to Islam. Over the coming centuries, power in the region was disputed between the Mongol chieftains, Persian princes and Turkish warlords who had also originally come from the east.

The Ottoman Turks captured Baghdad in 1534. For the next 300 years, local leaders opposed Turkish rule. But by 1834, the Ottoman Turks had gained control of the region that became the three **provinces** of Mosul, Baghdad and Basra, on the fringe of the **Ottoman Empire**.

THE OTTOMAN EMPIRE

The Ottoman Empire began in one of the Turkish states that sprang up in Anatolia (today the Asian part of modern Turkey). In 1453 CE the Ottomans conquered Byzantium, the last remaining part of the Roman Empire, and launched attacks on Europe. The Ottoman Turks adopted Constantinople as their capital, and renamed it Istanbul. The Ottomans dominated the Middle East for almost four centuries.

> **‟ These are lands great in extent, important by their position, once marvellously wealthy and still potentially so. ”**
> (Stephen Longrigg, a modern historian, writing about Iraq)

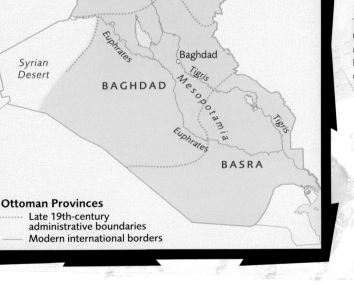

0 50 100 150 miles
0 80 160 240 km

N

Tigris

MOSUL

Syrian Desert

Euphrates

Baghdad

Tigris

BAGHDAD

Mesopotamia

Euphrates

Tigris

BASRA

This map shows the Ottoman provinces of Mosul, Baghdad and Basra, and the location of the city of Baghdad.

Ottoman Provinces
.... Late 19th-century administrative boundaries
——— Modern international borders

1921: Britain Creates the Kingdom of Iraq

In the early days of the 20th century, Arab **nationalists** within the Turkish-ruled Ottoman Empire began to believe that the Arabs had a right to live in countries of their own. The coming of World War I, which lasted from 1914 to 1918, gave the Arabs their chance, after the Turks decided to fight on Germany's side.

The British encouraged the Arab tribes of Arabia to revolt against the Turks and promised to help all the Arabs when the war was over. But at the same time, Great Britain and France secretly agreed to divide up the whole of the Middle East into zones that they would control. Iraq was to be controlled by Britain.

Baghdad in 1920, after a revolt against British rule.

> **There is still no Iraqi people, only masses lacking any patriotic ideal, connected by no common tie, prone to anarchy and always ready to rise up against any government whatsoever.** ""
>
> *(King Faisal of Iraq explains the problems of ruling the country)*

THE HASHEMITES

The Hashemite family of Mecca had for centuries held the post of Governor of Mecca under the Ottoman Turks. The head of the family during World War I was Sharif Hussein. His sons Faisal and Abdullah led the Arab revolt against the Turks. Faisal later became king of Iraq. Major T. E. Lawrence, who became known as 'Lawrence of Arabia', was the British officer sent to help organize the revolt.

After the war, the League of Nations, the international body set up by the winners of World War I to keep the peace, asked Britain to supervise Iraq and lead it to independence. This was known as the British **Mandate**. However, the population was made up of many different peoples, and Iraq was difficult to rule. In particular the Kurds in the northern province of Mosul wanted to be part of a separate country.

Britain decided Iraq would be more stable with a king. In 1921 the British chose King Faisal, from the family that had led the Arab revolt against the Turks. Meanwhile, the search for oil, which had begun before World War I, led to discoveries of large quantities in 1927.

The Monarchy 1921-1958

King Faisal was at first little known in Iraq. The British appointed Arab officials to run the country. Some were former Ottoman officials and others were Arab nationalists. Most were Sunni Muslims, despite the fact that most Iraqis were Shi'ites. Britain also chose an assembly to draft a **constitution**. British advisers played an important role.

In 1924 Iraq became a constitutional monarchy, where the king and an elected parliament each played a part. Treaties between Iraq and the UK ensured that the British continued to have a strong influence. In 1932 Iraq became independent, though the British continued to rule behind the scenes.

King Faisal died in 1933 and was succeeded by King Ghazi, who died in a car accident in 1939. His heir, King Faisal II, was only four years old, so a **regent** ruled on his behalf. In 1941, during World War II, politicians sympathetic to Nazi Germany rebelled. They formed a new government and appointed a different ruler. British forces quickly restored the former **regime**.

King Faisal II in 1945, when he was ten years old. He became king when he was four years old, and Iraq was ruled by a regent until Faisal II became eighteen.

After the war, Arab nationalists objected to the UK's attempt to negotiate a new treaty with Iraq. They also protested in 1955 against the pro-Western Baghdad Pact (see the panel on the right). Then, in 1958, to the surprise of the politicians and the royal family, there was a violent military **coup** led by General Qassem, a nationalist sympathetic to Egypt's President Nasser. Monarchy in Iraq came to a sudden and bloody end.

THE BAGHDAD PACT

The Baghdad Pact, as it became known, took shape in 1955, when Iraq signed a defence agreement with Turkey. Iran and Pakistan also joined the Pact, of which the UK was a leading member. The aim was to establish a defence system that would strengthen the Middle East against communist influence. Iraq left the Baghdad Pact in 1959, after the 1958 revolution.

❝ The Arabs have shown that they are united in their aims, despite imperialist attempts to sow [disagreement] amongst them. ❞
(Al-Ahram *newspaper, recalling the views of Egypt's President Nasser on the coup in Iraq)*

Iraq's Prime Minister Nuri al-Said speaks to the press before a meeting of the Baghdad Pact Council in April 1956.

In the Qassem coup of 1958, the King and a number of leading politicians, including Prime Minister Nuri al-Said, were killed. This brutality was new to Iraqi politics. General Qassem also had ruthless rivals. In 1959 a **Ba'athist** group tried to murder him, but failed. One of the would-be assassins was the young Saddam Hussein, who later had to flee the country.

General Qassem, who seized power on 14 July 1958. He believed the monarchy had not been in the interests of ordinary Iraqis.

Soon after gaining power, Qassem came into conflict with the West. In 1961 he stopped the British-owned Iraq Petroleum Company exploring for oil. He then set up the Iraqi National Oil Company. Qassem also took land from the big landowners to give to the poor farm workers. In 1961 Qassem claimed Kuwait was historically part of Iraq (see page 25). The UK took this threat seriously, and moved British troops into Kuwait for its protection. Qassem also alarmed the West by starting a friendly relationship with the Soviet Union, which gave Iraq weapons.

❝ Our revolution was not an accident: it was the outcome of careful planning and was based on Iraq's political needs. ❞
(General Qassem, 1958)

> **" How can a united nation be built, except by fierce struggle. Every Arab must seek in his heart to find the right way forwards. "**
> *(Ba'ath Party statement on how Arab peoples might be united)*

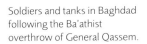

Soldiers and tanks in Baghdad following the Ba'athist overthrow of General Qassem.

In 1963 a group of anti-communist army officers, who were members of the **Ba'ath Party**, succeeded in overthrowing Qassem. However, the new president, Abdel-Salam Arif, soon left the Ba'ath Party. He then took personal control, and resumed links with Moscow. In 1968 yet another military coup brought the Ba'athists back to power, and President Hassan Bakr became leader of a new Ba'athist government.

THE BA'ATH PARTY
The Ba'ath Party was founded in Syria in the 1940s by Michael Aflaq and Salaheddin Bitar. The Arabic word Ba'ath means 'rebirth'. The party's aim is to achieve freedom and unity for the Arabs. There are groups of Ba'athists throughout the Arab world. The party came to power in Iraq, and also in Syria. Though the Ba'ath Party believes in democracy in theory, all Ba'athist rulers have been dictators.

President Bakr and the Ba'ath Party would rule Iraq for many years. Bakr's right-hand man was Saddam Hussein, whose role was to ensure that there would be no resistance to the regime. Saddam was the organizer and enforcer as the Ba'ath eliminated its opponents, executing or imprisoning all who might be a danger to it.

In 1972 Iraq took control of the foreign-owned Iraq Petroleum Company; in 1973 it would take complete control of its oil resources. Iraq was beginning to be a major oil producer. In 1972 the Ba'athists, who had opposed communism, signed a friendship treaty with the communist Soviet Union.

From 1973 onwards, Iraq was basically a dictatorship. The Ba'ath Party promised that democracy would eventually be restored, but this never happened. Membership of the Party grew. An increase in oil prices in 1973 gave Iraq an increased income, and Iraq began to prosper and flourish as a modern state.

IRAQ AND THE SOVIET UNION

The 1972 Treaty of Friendship with the Soviet Union meant Iraq got military and technical help from Moscow. At the time, the Soviet Union and the USA were engaged in the Cold War, a long period of antagonism. Choosing to side with the Soviet communists meant Iraq lost the sympathy of the USA.

Iraqi oil installations at Kirkuk in 1972. The country's oil industry was fully nationalized in 1973.

Despite the increased prosperity, there were troubles in northern Iraq, where the Kurds had never given up their ambition to have their own separate state. Many Kurds continued to want an independent country, called Kurdistan. In 1974 there was open war between the Kurds and the Baghdad government. Neither side won outright, and the resentment of the Kurds continued.

By the mid-1970s, President Bakr's health was not good. He began to withdraw from the leadership, as Saddam Hussein took greater control. Saddam began to increase his power by giving key positions to members of his family. He also appointed officials with whom he had tribal links, or a shared origin in the town of Tikrit. By 1977 most officials reported to Saddam Hussein. On 16 July 1979, Bakr resigned and Saddam Hussein took his place as president of Iraq.

❝ Iraq's former treaty with Britain was forced on the Iraqi people. Iraq's treaty with the Soviet Union is based on genuine shared interests. ❞

(Saddam Hussein, speaking in 1972)

This photograph, taken in 1976, shows then Vice President Saddam Hussein (seated on the left) with President Hassan Bakr to the right.

Saddam as President

In 1979 Saddam Hussein became president of the Iraqi Republic, secretary-general of the Ba'ath Party, chairman of the **Revolutionary Command Council** and commander-in-chief of Iraq's armed forces. He was in charge of a wealthy country. Iraq was not as rich as Saudi Arabia or Kuwait, but its oil revenues meant that everyone had jobs, while education and health services were free.

Saddam's first action was to eliminate all those who might oppose him. Five members of the 21-member Revolutionary Command Council were accused of treason and executed, along with 50 other senior leaders. Hundreds of junior officials were executed or dismissed.

Saddam Hussein also tried to attract popular support. He took a surprising step by deciding to restore Iraq's parliament, which had not met since 1958. However it was virtually impossible for anyone but a Ba'ath Party member to qualify to stand for membership of the new 250-member assembly, so the voters had little choice.

SADDAM HUSSEIN
Born on 28 April 1937, Saddam Hussein was brought up near the small town of Tikrit, raised by his uncle. In 1957 Saddam joined the Ba'ath Party and in 1959 took part in an attempt to murder Iraq's military ruler, General Qassem. He fled to Syria and then to Egypt, returning to Iraq in 1963 when the Ba'ath took power. He worked his way up through the ranks thanks to his closeness to Hassan Bakr, who became president in 1968.

Saddam Hussein takes his place on the international scene. Here, in 1979, as Iraq's new president, he attends the summit of non-aligned nations in Havana, Cuba.

Saddam also began to strengthen Iraq's army with all the modern arms he could get, some from the Soviet Union and some from the West. Iraq also began researching chemical and biological weapons. In addition Saddam pressed on with Iraq's nuclear research programme, buying uranium fuel. Western experts said Iraq's nuclear plans could only be aimed at building nuclear bombs.

SADDAM'S BRUTALITY

Saddam Hussein became known for his brutality. He personally killed many political opponents. At the same time, he began to develop a taste for extravagance. He built vast palaces, with ornate decor and furniture, living a life of luxury.

"With such a leader at its head, and with such wealth at its disposal, will Iraq now be able to revive its former glory?"
(Iraqi government statement on Saddam Hussein coming to power)

Iraq's military forces go on parade in Baghdad, under the triumphal arch of two swords designed by Saddam.

War with Iran

After Iran's Islamic Revolution of 1979, Saddam Hussein feared that Iran might stir up trouble in Iraq. Many Iraqis were Shi'ite Muslims, like the Iranians. They resented being ruled by Saddam's followers, who were mainly Sunni Muslims. Saddam also believed that so soon after the Islamic Revolution, Iran might be unprepared to defend itself.

Saddam wanted to seize the part of Iran next to Iraq, where many of the people spoke Arabic, and where Iran's oil resources were. He also wanted to get access to the entire waterway from Basra to the ocean, known as the Shatt el-Arab.

Iraqi troops attacked on 2 September 1980. Over the next eight years, war raged on. Iran surprised Iraq with the strength of its defence. Iranian troops crossed into Iraqi territory, and at one stage threatened the city of Basra. The two sides sank each other's ships in the Gulf, and aimed missiles at each other's cities. Saddam Hussein also attacked the Kurdish people inside Iraq, some of whom supported Iran.

Ayatollah Khomeini, the leader of Iran, speaks to his followers in Tehran in 1981.

> **When they realized it was a chemical attack [the people] tried to get out, but most of them died in the shelters.**
> *(Dana Nazif, a Kurdish resident of Halabja describes Saddam's attack on the city)*

Kurdish fighters inspect a chemical bomb dropped from an Iraqi aircraft during the 1988 raid on Halabja.

The Arab states of the Gulf supported Iraq with loans and **subsidies** during the war. Iraq's own oil revenues suffered, and much of its remaining income was spent on the war. The West also supported Iraq. Arab and Western support was a result of fear that the Islamic Revolution in Iran might spread, threatening the existing governments in the region. From 1982 the USA and other Western countries gave economic support to Iraq, and supplied weapons and intelligence. In March 1988 Saddam Hussein ordered a chemical attack on Kurds in the northern Iraqi town of Halabja, killing 5,000 people. The USA expressed horror at the act at the time, but soon began to support Saddam Hussein once more.

The war did not go well for Iraq, and Saddam Hussein declared that it was over in August 1988. The major result of the war was that Iraq had sacrificed much of its former prosperity and was deeply in debt, especially to its oil-producing Arab neighbours, who had helped to fund the war.

SADDAM HUSSEIN AND WEAPONS OF MASS DESTRUCTION

Chemical weapons were developed by Iraq during the war with Iran, and were used against the Kurds and at the battlefront. Iraq also planned to develop biological weapons. But Saddam Hussein's big plan was to produce a nuclear weapon. This scheme was halted in June 1981, when Israeli warplanes destroyed Iraq's nuclear research reactor, 'Osiraq', near Baghdad.

23

1990: The Invasion of Kuwait

After the end of the war with Iran, Saddam Hussein was furious with his Arab neighbours. He believed Iraq should not have to pay its debts, since Iraq had defended its neighbours from Iran. He also needed cash from Iraq's oil revenue, and accused Kuwait in particular of driving the oil price down by producing too much oil.

To the world's astonishment, Iraq invaded Kuwait in the early hours of the morning on 2 August 1990. (Saddam had previously said that he would *not* attack Kuwait.) There was little resistance. The ruler of Kuwait fled to Saudi Arabia. Iraq declared Kuwait to be its own territory. Saddam's plan was that Iraq would no longer need to pay its debt to Kuwait, and would have Kuwait's oil revenue for itself.

Only in the Arab world was there any support for Saddam Hussein. Some individual Arabs believed the Kuwaiti ruling family had been keeping oil money selfishly for their own use. Yemen and Sudan expressed support for Iraq, while Jordan remained neutral.

Iraqi tanks in Kuwait City on the morning of 2 August 1990.

29 August 1990: refugees in Amman, Jordan. Refugees of all nationalities fled from Kuwait and Iraq after the war began.

In Washington, US President George H. W. Bush announced he would not permit what he called 'naked **aggression**'. Other countries around the world also called on Iraq to withdraw. Up until 1990 the USA had not opposed Saddam Hussein, and he was surprised by the American reaction.

Some Kuwaitis who had fled the country made accusations that Iraqi troops had committed brutal attacks on the people while they held Kuwait. Most of these accusations were later found to be false. However, homes and offices were looted, while the citizens of Kuwait were terrified and soon began to run short of food and other necessities.

IRAQ'S CLAIM TO KUWAIT

Kuwait was once part of the Ottoman province of Basra, which later became part of Iraq. In November 1914, after the outbreak of World War I, Great Britain recognized Kuwait as an independent state under British protection. But Saddam argued that Kuwait should have remained part of Iraq, like the rest of Basra Province. After the invasion he declared Kuwait to be Iraq's 19th province.

1991: Iraq Driven Out of Kuwait

The USA said its view on the Iraqi occupation of Kuwait was that international law must be observed, and no state may take the territory of another.

US President George H. W. Bush persuaded many countries, including the UK and some Arab states, to join a military **coalition** to drive the Iraqis out. Many around the world believed the real issue was control of Kuwait's **oil reserves**. If Saddam had been able to combine the Kuwaiti oil reserves with those of Iraq, he would have been in control of a very large proportion of the world's oil.

> **❝ I will not allow this little dictator to control 25 per cent of the civilized world's oil. ❞**
> (George H. W. Bush, speaking to King Hussein of Jordan, August 1990)

US President George H. W. Bush and the Commander of the allied forces, US General Norman Schwarzkopf, in Saudi Arabia in November 1990.

Black smoke billows from a burning oil field in Kuwait, set alight by the fleeing Iraqi troops.

Saddam refused to withdraw his troops. In February 1991 the USA began a long bombardment of Iraqi positions in Kuwait and in Iraq itself. On 24 February 1991, the Coalition forces, under the command of US General Norman Schwarzkopf, attacked the remaining Iraqi troops in Kuwait. The attack was called Operation Desert Storm. The Iraqis offered little resistance, but set Kuwait's oil wells alight as they left. The USA estimated that 100,000 Iraqi troops were killed in the fighting.

A **ceasefire** was declared by the Coalition after four days. On 3 March the Iraqi military commanders accepted the terms put to them by the Coalition forces. The USA decided not to pursue the Iraqi troops back into Iraq. The reason given much later by the Coalition leadership was that if the Iraqi government were overthrown, it would be difficult to cope with the resulting situation in Iraq.

THE KURDS REBEL

After the Iraqi invasion of Kuwait, the Kurds of northern Iraq rose up against Saddam Hussein and declared themselves autonomous. Thousands of Kurds were killed by Iraqi forces and many fled. The UN then said there should be safe havens for the Kurds, and that the USA and the UK should protect them from Saddam Hussein. Under the protection of allied planes, the Kurds created an autonomous zone. In the south, however, no protection was given to the Shi'ites, and Saddam Hussein brutally suppressed a Shi'ite uprising.

1991-2001: Sanctions and the Effects

After the war the United Nations passed **Security Council Resolution** 687. This laid down rules for Iraq. Iraq had to respect the international frontier with Kuwait, give up its banned weapons and pay compensation to Kuwait and other parties that had been harmed.

Though Iraq did not use chemical or biological weapons in the war over Kuwait, the fear remained that it possessed them. Security Council Resolution 687, passed in April 1991, said that Iraq could no longer trade until it got rid of its weapons of mass destruction and its missiles. Iraq was also supposed to pay compensation for damage done to Kuwait, and for losses of oil revenue. Until these conditions were met, Iraq was only allowed to import food and some other essentials. This meant that Iraq could no longer freely export oil and had little or no income.

UNITED NATIONS RESOLUTION 687
'Iraq must accept the destruction or removal of all nuclear material, chemical and biological weapons and ballistic missiles with ranges greater than 150 km (93 mi). The United Nations will monitor the destruction and removal of weapons.'

A Baghdad hospital in April 1991. Sanctions made it difficult to care for Iraq's children.

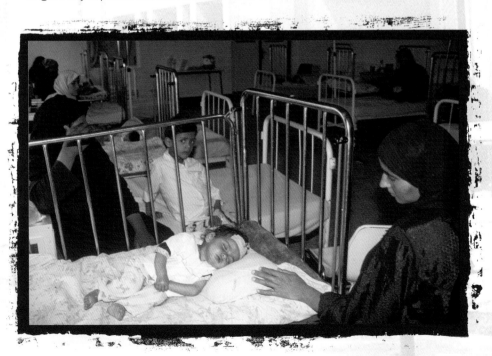

Under the sanctions, Iraq's previously high standard of living dropped sharply. The country lost almost all oil income. The sanctions were modified when the United Nations set up an Oil-for-Food Programme in 1995. Under this plan, accepted by Iraq, the country could export oil to pay for food and medical supplies. The Oil-for-Food Programme improved the situation for ordinary Iraqis, but some of the money was not spent on food and medicine for the Iraqi people. Food had to be rationed, and many Iraqis lost their jobs. **Inflation** also reduced the value of people's incomes. Children in particular suffered. The **child mortality rate** rose, and schools and hospitals found it difficult to keep going.

The sanctions had a serious effect on ordinary Iraqis. However, many people also believe that the Iraqi government could have done more to help its people. Instead it spent too much of its money on Saddam Hussein's own projects and for military purposes.

❝ There is a human calamity going on in Iraq ... caused by US-driven economic sanctions. ❞
(Dennis Halliday, former United Nations humanitarian coordinator in Iraq)

❝ Those who believed in sanctions underestimated the Iraqi will to resist. ❞
(Paul D. Taylor, US Naval War College)

Sajjud Palace, Baghdad, one of Saddam's many palaces.

1991-2002: The No-fly Zones

During the period from 1991 onwards, 'no-fly zones' were established over northern and southern Iraq. Iraqi planes were forbidden to fly and help Iraq's forces attack the Kurds or Shi'ites from the air. This operation was carried out by the USA and the UK, not the United Nations.

The no-fly zones were policed by American and British planes. They flew from bases in Turkey in the north and from aircraft carriers in the Gulf in the south. Iraqi planes were not allowed to fly south of the **latitude** 33 degrees north (which cuts across Iraq just south of Baghdad) or north of the latitude 36 degrees north. The operation was given the title 'Provide Comfort'.

The no-fly zones were intended to protect those parts of Iraq's population that had mounted uprisings in 1991 after the US-led coalition had driven the Iraqis from Kuwait. These people were vulnerable to attack by Saddam Hussein's forces.

The southern zone gave some protection to the Shi'ite population. Iraq was allowed to use helicopters, however, and it used these to suppress a Shi'ite uprising in 1991. In the north, the Kurds did better. The no-fly zone protected the Kurdish autonomous area set up after 1991, allowing the Kurds to establish a government of their own.

Kurdish 'Peshmerga' fighters, meaning 'Those who face death', in the Kurdish area of northern Iraq.

During the period from the end of the war to 1998, US and UK planes flying in the no-fly zones attacked Iraqi aircraft, and also radar stations on the ground. These attacks became more severe and happened more often after Iraq's announcement in 1998 that it would no longer recognize the existence of the zones, which it thought interfered with Iraq's national rights. After Operation Desert Fox in 1998 (see pages 32–33), Iraq began to fire missiles at US and UK planes in the zones, whose attacks on ground targets in the no-fly zones increased.

(see pages 32–33)

AUTONOMY FOR THE KURDS

In October 1991 the Iraqi Government voluntarily withdrew from the Kurdish region of the country. The Kurds were left to govern themselves. Elections were held in May 1992 to elect a Kurdish parliament, and the Kurdish area set up its own regional government.

No-fly Zones, August 1992–March 2003
▢ No-fly zones

❝ Immediately after the Gulf War, during Operation Provide Comfort, the goal was to protect the Kurds, but what we're doing now is enforcing the no-fly zone. ❞
(USAF pilot)

This map shows the latitude lines, known as the 36th and 32nd parallels, that mark the northern and southern no-fly zones.

1991-2001: Sanctions and the Inspections

After Iraq's forces had been expelled from Kuwait, the United Nations sent in teams of weapons inspectors to check whether Saddam Hussein had destroyed his banned weapons. Despite much effort from the inspectors, no weapons of mass destruction were found.

In 1991 the United Nations had set up UNSCOM (United Nations Special Commission) to search Iraq for forbidden weapons. Saddam Hussein's officials gave UNSCOM little help. Saddam later claimed that he had disposed of his weapons of mass destruction in 1991, but did not wish to admit this as he thought it would make him appear weak in the eyes of his neighbours, especially Iran.

In 1998 Iraq completely stopped co-operating with UNSCOM after it refused to agree that there were no weapons. UNSCOM pulled out of Iraq. In December 1998 Iraq declared it would withdraw all co-operation unless the UN considered lifting the sanctions, adding that it would also cease to recognize the no-fly zones. In retaliation, US President Bill Clinton launched four days of air attacks on Iraq. This was the start of what was known as Operation Desert Fox.

UN weapons inspectors set off under the watchful eyes of an Iraqi sentry in December 1998.

A UN resolution in December 1999 set up a new organization, UNMOVIC (United Nations Monitoring Inspection and Verification Commission). For three years Iraq refused to let UNMOVIC carry out inspections, changing its mind only in late 2002.

Before the invasion of Kuwait, Iraq certainly did have weapons of mass destruction. There have been suggestions that these may remain hidden, or could have been sent to another country. Most likely, they were destroyed as Saddam Hussein has claimed.

SADDAM HUSSEIN'S MURDEROUS REGIME

The USA has accused Saddam of killing 300,000 of his own citizens.

• Roughly 180,000 Kurds died in 1988 when they were suspected of co-operating with Iran.

• At least 60,000 Shi'ites died when Saddam repressed their uprising against him in 1991.

• Another 60,000 people who died were political prisoners and others killed by Saddam's regime over the 25 years when he ran the country.

Hundreds of thousands of Iraqis also died as soldiers in the Iraq-Iran war.

❝ If Saddam defies the world and we fail to respond, we will face a far greater threat in the future. ❞
(US President Clinton, speaking about Operation Desert Fox)

Inspectors of the UN organization UNSCOM prepare banned Iraqi missiles for destruction.

11 September: A Turning Point

The World Trade Center, about to be hit by a second aircraft, during the 11 September attacks on the USA.

On 11 September 2001, hijacked aircraft destroyed the Twin Towers of the World Trade Center building in New York. The Pentagon was also hit, and one aircraft crashed in Pennsylvania. It is believed that the US Capitol Building was the intended target of the Pennsylvania aircraft. The response of President George W. Bush was to call for a 'War on Terror', though no target was immediately in view. Iraq was at first not mentioned.

On 16 September Vice President Dick Cheney said there was no evidence of any Iraqi involvement in the attacks. Instead responsibility was soon given to Osama bin Laden and his Al-Qaeda terrorist network. On 3 October Deputy Secretary of State Richard Armitage said that it was clear that bin Laden was to blame.

The USA reacted with an attack on Afghanistan, where bin Laden was based. On 7 October US bombs began to fall on targets in that country. By December 2001 Afghan opposition forces had ousted the **Taliban** regime, which had supported Osama bin Laden. Bin Laden himself had disappeared from view, and US special forces in Afghanistan failed to find him.

US special forces in Afghanistan search mountain caves for Osama bin Laden in 2002.

> **The United States certainly does not have the option of doing nothing about Saddam Hussein.** *(President George W. Bush's Secretary of State and former national security adviser, Condoleeza Rice)*

In January 2002 President Bush made a speech that named Iraq, along with Iran and North Korea, as a member of what the President called an 'Axis of Evil', because they were alleged to support terrorism. Throughout 2002 the USA continued to stress what it said was the danger to the world from Iraq.

On 16 September 2002, after President Bush's speech of 12 September to the United Nations (see page 36), Saddam Hussein suddenly invited the UN arms inspectors to return. UNMOVIC began work in November 2002. By this stage, however, it had begun to seem likely that President Bush's aim was to get rid of Saddam Hussein and replace his government with a different one. However, this was not yet official policy.

THE NEO-CONSERVATIVES AND IRAQ

Amongst President Bush's policy advisers was a group known as the neo-conservatives. These advisers supported a US foreign policy of bringing change to parts of the world hostile to the USA by installing pro-Western, democratic governments.

Iraq and the United Nations

One way in which the USA stepped up the pressure on Iraq was through the United Nations. President Bush spoke to the UN General Assembly on 12 September 2002. He accused Iraq of failing to comply with UN Security Council resolutions and of supporting terrorism. However, he did not accuse Saddam Hussein directly of any part in the 11 September attacks.

On 8 November 2002, the UN Security Council passed Resolution 1441, condemning Iraq's failure to comply with previous resolutions. The USA and the UK had managed to get the approval of the other permanent members of the Security Council.

President George W. Bush addressing the UN General Assembly on 12 September 2002.

INTERNATIONAL ATTITUDES TO IRAQ

In Europe some governments supported President Bush's aims in Iraq. In the UK, Prime Minister Tony Blair agreed that British troops would join any invasion force. But many ordinary people disagreed and there were huge demonstrations against the war, in both the UK and the USA. Other countries, notably France, opposed the USA. Most Arab countries also opposed the invasion of Iraq.

An anti-war demonstration in New York's Central Park on 6 October 2002.

> **" France is not anti-American. But we just feel that there is another option than war... And we should pursue it until there is no more hope. "**
> (President Jacques Chirac of France, 16 March 2003)

The terms of Resolution 1441 strongly disapproved of the Iraqi government's actions. However, it was deliberately phrased so that it could not be seen as justifying military action against Iraq unless another resolution specifically said this should happen. Iraq was instructed to produce within 30 days a document saying what it had done with its weapons. This document was handed over on 7 December 2002. By then, however, the USA had decided that only military action could end what it said was the danger from Iraq. But UN backing for war could not be obtained, since France and Russia were unwilling to agree.

> **" The war in Iraq is in danger of rocking global stability and the foundations of international law. "**
> (President Vladimir Putin of Russia, 28 March 2003)

The Invasion of Iraq

On 17 March 2003, US President Bush made a speech giving Saddam Hussein 48 hours to leave the country, or war would begin. The UNMOVIC weapons inspectors left Iraq on 18 March. On 20 March hostilities began, with an air attack on Baghdad. 'Operation Iraqi Freedom', as the campaign was named, was under way.

The invading forces entered Iraq from Kuwait in the south. The Turkish government refused to allow a US force to enter Iraq from the north. The early stages of the invasion did not go as quickly as planned. The Iraqi port of Umm Qasr, on Iraq's tiny coastline at the head of the Gulf, did not fall for a week. Units of the Iraqi army, though separated from each other, continued to fight the invasion, as did some armed civilians.

The superior firepower of the invading coalition troops meant they were soon victorious, however. Baghdad fell on 9 April. On 1 May, President Bush declared that the war was over. People in the northern Kurdish areas were happy. However, most Iraqis were not openly enthusiastic. In other parts of the world, many people still thought the war was wrong.

> ❝ The Iraqi people tried but failed to remove Saddam Hussein for 35 years. It was a difficult task, and we thank the Americans. ❞
>
> *(Sayyed Bashir al-Musawi, an Iraqi cleric in northern Baghdad, 20 May 2003)*

British soldiers check local people on the road to Basra.

IRAQI RESISTANCE

The Iraqi resistance included units of the regular army, as well as paramilitary forces. The Iraqi government had given weapons to Ba'athist supporters and other militias before the invasion. Many resistance fighters were killed, but there were few coalition casualties.

Chaos reigned for Iraqi civilians, and there were many civilian casualties. Law and order broke down, and kidnapping and score-settling soon began. Looting also broke out. Iraqi government offices were stripped, with little attempt by the coalition troops to protect them. The Iraqi Museum was looted, though it was later discovered that museum staff had successfully hidden many treasures. In addition, services such as electricity, water and sewage disposal, which were already neglected by the Iraqi government during sanctions, became even worse.

> ❝ It really hurts to see the lack of security. I don't see the British doing anything about it. There are far too many guns around. ❞
>
> (Anonymous former Iraqi policeman, 14 May 2003)

After the fall of Baghdad, many local people looted everything they could from government buildings.

Sunnis, Kurds and Shi'ites

The aftermath of the invasion has drawn attention to the divisions between Iraq's different communities. Many people ask whether these communities can continue to live together, and whether they will be able to forge a new country out of the ruins of the old Iraq.

The main splits in Iraq are between the Kurds in the north, the Sunni Muslims in the centre and the Shi'ites in the south. This is a simplified description, since there are members of every community in every part of the country. In addition, between 5 and 10 per cent of Iraqis belong to smaller groups, including Arab Christians.

> **❝ Each community will try to get as much power and territory as it can. ❞**
> *(Ayatollah Mohammed Taqi al-Muddaresi, a senior Shi'ite cleric)*

The Sunni Muslims have been the ruling group in Iraq for many years, as Saddam Hussein's supporters were a Sunni group. Sunnis make up only 20 per cent of the Arab population of Iraq, however. Most of the Kurds are also Sunnis (with a few Shi'ites), but see themselves as separate from the Arabs.

Shi'ite Muslims in Baghdad in January 2004 show posters of their leader, Grand Ayatollah Ali al-Sistani.

Almost 60 per cent of Iraqis are Shi'ite Muslims, like many people who live in neighbouring Iran. The Shi'ites were expected to welcome the invasion, but they have been less satisfied than was anticipated. In the new Iraq, the Shi'ites want recognition for the fact that they are the majority. Many follow religious leaders, such as Ayatollah Ali al-Sistani, who has tried to ease the conflicts between the invading forces and Shi'ite Muslim groups. However, some Shi'ites want the new Iraq to be a Muslim religious state. This would probably not fit in with the Western-style democracy desired by the USA and its allies.

Around 18 per cent of Iraqis are Kurdish. The Kurds now fear that they may lose their autonomy. They would like to control the northern city of Kirkuk, which they think of as their capital, and to have part of Iraq's oil resources for themselves.

Kurdish demonstrators in the city of Kirkuk demand a federal state.

RIVAL VIEWPOINTS

Some Kurds demand a federal system of government in Iraq, in which regional assemblies would control each area. The Kurds have already experienced autonomy within Iraq, during the 12 years when Saddam Hussein was prevented from interfering in the Kurdish area.

In contrast the Shi'ites favour a single Arab state, which would give them a dominant position because they are the largest single group.

❝ We cannot take our proposal for autonomy to an Iraqi assembly. It would be killed off, because we are a minority. ❞
(Hoshyar Zebari, Iraqi foreign minister, who is a Kurd)

2003-2004: Resistance Continues

While most Iraqis were relieved that Saddam Hussein's government had been overthrown, resistance to the American forces carried on through 2003 and 2004. This was in spite of the fact that elections were due to take place in January 2005.

In May 2003 the occupying forces set up a body called the **Coalition Provisional Authority**, headed by Paul Bremer, an American **diplomat**. The Coalition Provisional Authority governed the country. The US authorities also appointed an Iraqi advisory body, the Iraqi Governing Council.

However, these political bodies could not stop the violence. Throughout 2003 and into 2004, attacks on the occupying forces became increasingly regular. According to the **interim** Iraqi authorities and US officials, these attacks were the work of former Ba'athists, religious fanatics and foreign fighters.

Some Iraqis condemned the continued violence. A large number of Iraqis, however, believed that the reason behind the attacks was the refusal of many people to tolerate continued foreign occupation. There were especially violent scenes in the Shi'ite holy city of Najaf and the Sunni stronghold of Fallujah.

IRAQI CASUALTIES
In October 2004 a study by US scientists said that 100,000 Iraqis had died as a result of the war. Previous estimates of civilian deaths (from violence, not including disease and other health problems) had suggested a minimum figure of 15,000. Just over 1,000 US soldiers had died in the same period.

" What they [the invading forces] have achieved is chaos, collective punishment, assassinations, the torture of prisoners and the destruction of the country's infrastructure. **"**
(Haifa Zangana, Iraqi-born novelist, 25 October 2004)

As the violence went on, Iraq's basic services such as electricity and water were not fully repaired. There was also widespread unemployment, while many people felt threatened by the increasing violence and lawlessness.

As time passed, the violence seemed only to intensify. There were kidnappings of Iraqis and foreigners, and some kidnap victims were killed. Suicide bombings began to be a daily event, and happened even next to the so-called Green Zone in Baghdad, where the Coalition Provisional Authority was based. Many of the Iraqis who were killed were those who had been co-operating with the US forces, particularly recruits to the new police force. In December 2004 a suicide bomb at a US base in Mosul killed 23 people, including 19 Americans.

❝ A free Iraq will be a decisive blow to terrorism and a victory for the civilized world and for the security of America. ❞
(*President George W. Bush, 1 June 2004*)

The horrendous aftermath of a suicide bombing in Najaf on 20 December 2004.

Interim Government

In the second half of 2004, Iraq entered a new phase. The US-led occupying forces attempted to put a final end to resistance and violence in the country, in preparation for elections in January 2005. The first step was to give more power to Iraqis.

On 1 June 2004, the Coalition Provisional Authority ceased to exist. An assembly of 1,000 influential Iraqis then chose the members of the Iraqi Interim Government. This new government, in theory, now ruled over Iraq. Dr Ayad Allawi, a Shi'ite, became the interim prime minister.

American officials continued to be closely involved in the running of the country. The American forces consulted with the Iraqi Interim Government, but they did not take direct orders from it.

AYAD ALLAWI

Dr Ayad Allawi, Iraq's interim prime minister, was born in 1945. As a young man, he joined the Ba'ath Party. In 1971 he moved to London to continue his medical studies, and resigned from the Ba'ath in 1975. In 1978 an attempt was made to murder him. In 1990 he founded an Iraqi opposition group in exile called the Iraqi National Accord. He had links with the intelligence services in the UK and the USA.

Dr Ayad Allawi (left), the interim prime minister of Iraq, with US President George W. Bush at the White House in 2004.

Security continued to be a problem. The US occupying forces fired all Ba'ath Party members, so the government had to rely on inexperienced police recruits. These new recruits were regularly attacked by forces opposed to the invasion of Iraq and many were killed in car bombings and other attacks. Some former Ba'athists were later allowed to work for the new authorities.

Meanwhile temporary solutions were found to some security problems. Shi'ite violence in the holy city of Najaf was stopped after an agreement was reached with Shi'ite leader Moqtada al-Sadr. Violence in Sadr City, the Shi'ite suburb of Baghdad, was also brought to an end. The US military and the Interim Government also agreed on the need to halt Sunni resistance in Fallujah. American officials said the order for an assault on Fallujah had to come from the Iraqis. The attack on Fallujah began in November 2004.

❝ The terrorists and insurgents continue to use Fallujah and the Fallujah people as a shield for their murderous acts... I cannot stand back and allow such attacks to continue. ❞
(Iraqi interim Prime Minister Dr Ayad Allawi, October 2004)

This masked militia man holds a rocket brought into an army post in the Shi'ite Baghdad suburb known as Sadr City, in response to the Interim Government's call for an arms amnesty.

Turbulent Iraq

Iraq's future depends on its security. Unless the violence in Iraq ends, it will be difficult for the oil industry to recover. Without the income from oil, the government will find it hard to get Iraq's schools, hospitals, roads and railways working again.

There are some good things about Iraq's situation. Few people miss Saddam Hussein. The country is on the road to democracy. However, many blame the occupying forces for the continuing violence and civilian deaths. The USA hoped that, following Iraq's democratic elections of 2005, violence would decrease, but this did not happen immediately.

One ongoing problem is that few Sunni Muslims have become involved in the new government of Iraq. Many of Saddam's supporters were Sunnis, and their dislike of the Shi'ite majority meant that many refused to vote in 2005. Instead, Sunni terrorists have launched suicide bombings, and regular kidnappings and murders of civilians. The terrorists have also targeted Iraq's new police force, with many recruits and officers being killed.

An Iraqi protests against the kidnapping of aid worker Margaret Hassan in October 2004. Mrs Hassan, who had lived in Iraq for 30 years and was married to an Iraqi, was murdered shortly after.

❝ While there is no single root cause of terrorism, perceived humiliation and a lack of political and economic opportunities make young men susceptible to extremism. This can evolve easily into violence. ❞
(Harvard University terrorism expert Jessica Stern)

Iraqis in Najaf wave their voting registration papers. The election for the Transitional National Assembly was held on 30 January 2005. Shi'ites gained the most votes.

Without an effective police force, recovery and democracy will be extremely difficult for Iraq. In each bombing incident, many of the dead are recruits to Iraq's new security forces, but most are innocent civilians. Kidnappings by criminals are common. Many Iraqis who can afford to are leaving the country, especially Iraq's Christians.

Iraq's economy suffered because of the old UN sanctions regime, and continues to struggle today. By 2003 work and business had virtually stopped. Though there was some recovery after the invasion, unemployment was still widespread and pay was low. Iraq's oil industry continued to run at a reduced level, and there were regular attacks on the oil pipelines. The recovery of Iraq looks like being a long and difficult process.

❝ Civilian deaths have always been a tragic reality of modern war. But the conflict in Iraq was supposed to be different... US and UK forces were dispatched to liberate the Iraqi people, not to impose their own tyranny of violence. ❞
(Scott Ritter, former UN weapons inspector, and US marine)

Glossary

Abbasid dynasty dynasty of Caliphs who ruled in Baghdad from 749 CE to 1258 CE

aggression attacking something or someone for no reason

autonomous, autonomy having self government, but in general within another country rather than in a separate state

Ba'ath Party non-religious political party founded in Syria in the 1940s, but also strong in Iraq. It is based on Arab nationalism and socialism. Ba'athism's founder, Michael Aflaq, was a Christian. Both Muslims and Christians have been Ba'athists. Unfortunately, Ba'athist governments have always been led by dictators.

Ba'athists Ba'ath means rebirth. Ba'athists are members of the Ba'ath Party.

biological weapons weapons that cause harm by releasing dangerous germs or viruses

Caliph successor to the Prophet Mohammed as the leader of the Muslim community. There is no Caliph today.

ceasefire when fighting nations or groups agree to momentarily stop fighting

chemical weapons weapons that cause harm by releasing dangerous chemicals. Modern chemical weapons damage a victim's nervous system, causing rapid death.

child mortality rate number of children who die, normally expressed as the number of deaths per 1,000 live births

cleric minister of religion. In Islam clerics have no particular ceremony in which they become men of God. They reach their position through devotion to God and learning, causing other clerics and ordinary people to accept them.

coalition when countries work together to achieve a common goal

Coalition Provisional Authority government body set up in 2003 by the victorious allies, led by the USA, to govern Iraq

communist person who believes in a system of government in which a single party controls everything and there is no private property

Constantinople name of the great city that was the capital of the Roman Empire of the East. The Greeks called it Byzantium and the Turks renamed it Istanbul, which is its modern name.

constitution document containing all the legal rules under which a country is governed. A constitution also sets out the powers of the different parts of the government in relation to each other.

coup violent action that leads to a change in government. Coups are mainly, but not always, carried out by the military.

democracy system in which the people of a country hold elections to choose who their government leaders will be. In a democratic country, there is also in general what is known as the rule of law. This means the government cannot do what it likes, but must obey the laws.

dictator ruler who orders people to do what he wishes, and does not consult the people about what they want

diplomat person who works out and negotiates issues between nations

inflation when a country's currency loses its value, and more money is needed to buy goods. If wages do not rise, people become poorer.

insurgent person who tries to overthrow an established government by violence, for whatever reason

interim refers to something temporary, meant only for a limited time rather than permanently

irrigating, irrigation to supply land with water by artificial means

Kurds people who live mainly in northern Iraq and some other surrounding countries. They are a minority in Iraq.

latitude horizontal lines around the earth specified by a number of degrees north or south of the Equator

mandate arrangement where a developed country became a kind of caretaker, looking after a new country until it was supposedly ready for independence

Mesopotamia old name for what became Iraq. It means 'the land between the rivers'.

minorities small parts of a population that differ from the main part (majority) in some characteristics. Minorities are sometimes treated badly by the majority.

nationalist member of a political party or group who wants an independent nation

neo-conservative refers to a number of US foreign policy advisers who favour an active American foreign policy intended to spread democracy and pro-American attitudes in the world by whatever means necessary

oil reserves the total amount of oil that a country has that is still in the ground

Ottoman Empire Turkish Empire that dominated the Middle East for four centuries until its disappearance at the end of World War I

province separate district or area of a country

regent person who holds royal power temporarily while waiting for an infant monarch to become an adult. Iraq had a regent from 1939 to 1953.

regime government in power

Revolutionary Command Council (RCC) expression used to describe a group of senior officers who help govern a country where the president has come to power in a military coup. General Qassem appointed an RCC in Iraq, and there continued to be an RCC under Saddam Hussein.

sanctions form of punishment, where the United Nations bans a country from trading or from other activities in order to force it to obey a UN resolution

Security Council resolution formal decision to take action against a nation or group that is breaking international law. It is voted on by the UN Security Council (see United Nations).

Shi'ite Muslims members of the Shi'a sect of Islam. 60 per cent of Iraqis are Shi'ites (see Sunni Muslims).

subsidies money given to a person, private company or nation to assist in an activity that is good for the general public

Sunni Muslims the split between Sunni and Shi'ite dates back to the early days of Islam, when the Prophet's cousin and son-in-law, Ali, challenged Mu'awiya for the position of Caliph. The Sunnis were the mainstream, while the Shi'ites, who followed Ali, believed a Caliph should be a descendant of Mohammed. The Sunnis and Shi'ites have different religious practices, but both stand by the basic principles of Islam.

Taliban hard-line Sunni Muslim rulers of Afghanistan. They were overthrown in December 2001.

United Nations (UN) all countries are members of this organization. Its job is to try to keep the peace in the world. The body within the UN that passes resolutions that members must obey is called the Security Council. The Security Council has fifteen members. Five of these (the UK, the USA, France, Russia and China) are permanent members. The other ten members are taken from the entire membership of the United Nations, with each country serving for a two-year period.

weapons of mass destruction (WMD) normally means nuclear, chemical and biological weapons, used to kill as many people as possible at once

IRAQ

GEOGRAPHY

Location: Middle East, bordering the Gulf, west of Iran

Area: 437,072 square kilometres (168,000 square miles). This is slightly more than twice the size of Idaho, and 20% smaller than France.

Land borders: Jordan, Syria, Turkey, Iran, Kuwait and Saudi Arabia

Climate: Extreme. Winter is cool in the south, harsh in the north. Summer temperatures in the south can rise extremely high to over 48 °C.

Land use:

Arable land	14%
Uncultivated	86%

The land is mainly desert.

POPULATION

Population size:	26,074,906

Age structure:

0–14 years	40%
15–64 years	57%
65 years and above	3%

Median age:	19.4 years
Population growth rate:	2.7%

Life expectancy at birth:

Total population	68.7 years
Male	67.5 years
Female	70.0 years

Ethnic groups:

Arabs	75–80%
Kurds	15–20%
Others	5%

Religions:

Muslim	97%
(consisting of Shi'ite	60–65%
and Sunni	32–37%)
Christian and other	3%

Literacy rate (age 15 years and over):

Total population	40%
Male	56%
Female	24%

ECONOMY

Iraq's economy depends on oil, which has traditionally provided 95% of Iraq's foreign earnings. International sanctions since 1991 have severely limited Iraq's earnings from this source and the oil infrastructure has been damaged since the US-led invasion in 2003. Rebuilding of oil, electricity and other infrastructure is under way, but is hampered by the insurgency.

GDP:	US$89.8 billion
GDP growth rate:	52.3%
GDP per capita (at purchasing power parity):	US$3,500

This figure means that the GDP per capita in Iraq in local currency would buy the same quantity of goods as would US$3,500 spent in the USA.

GDP by sector:

Agriculture	13.6%
Industry	58.6%
Services	27.8%

Oil production: 2.25 million barrels per day
Pre-war production under sanctions restrictions (2002) was 2.8 million barrels per day.

Oil reserves:	112.5 billion barrels
Inflation rate:	25.4%
Labour force:	6.7 million

A post-war economic shutdown in many sectors in Iraq means that unemployment remains very high.

(*Source:* CIA World Factbook, 2005)

Timeline

1910–1990

1910

1917 British troops occupy Baghdad

1920

1920 League of Nations Mandate over Iraq given to Great Britain. Anti-British uprising.
1921 Faisal I becomes King

1930

1932 Iraq becomes independent, signs treaty with the UK
1933 King Ghazi takes the throne
1937 Saddam Hussein born in Tikrit
1939 Death of King Ghazi, succeeded by King Faisal II (aged 4)

1940

1941 Coup by Rashid Ali Gailani, overthrown by return of British forces

1945 Iraq joins Arab League

1948 Iraq takes part in fight against Israel

1950

1953 Faisal II begins his rule
1955 Iraq signs Baghdad Pact alliance

1958 Iraqi government overthrown by military coup led by General Qassem. King Faisal II is killed, with other leading figures.

1960

1963 First Ba'ath Party coup by Colonel Arif. General Qassem executed.

1968 Second Ba'athist coup brings President Bakr to power

1970

1979 Saddam Hussein takes over from Bakr
1980 Iran-Iraq war begins

1980

1988 Saddam Hussein attacks the Kurds with chemical weapons in Halabja
1988 Iran-Iraq war ends

1990

1990–2005

1990

1990 2 Aug.: Iraq invades Kuwait
6 Aug.: United Nations imposes first sanctions on Iraq

1991 16 Jan.: Gulf War begins with air strikes on Iraq
27 Feb.: US-led alliance drives Iraqi troops out of Kuwait
3 Mar.: Iraq accepts ceasefire
6 Apr.: Iraq accepts UN resolution, setting up weapons inspections to make sure it has destroyed its banned weapons
10 Apr.: 'Safe haven' established in northern Iraq for the Kurds

1992 26 Apr.: The USA and the UK establish no-fly zone in southern Iraq

1995

1995 14 Apr.: UN Oil-for-Food Programme begins, enabling Iraq to sell oil to buy food and medicine

1998 13 Dec.: Iraq first withdraws co-operation from UN inspectors.
16 Dec.: UN inspectors withdraw from Iraq and Operation Desert Fox begins, when the USA and the UK bomb Iraqi targets

2000

2001

2001 15 Feb.: More air attacks on Iraq after Iraq air defences threaten UK and US planes

2002

2002 30 Jan.: US President George W. Bush says Iraq is part of Axis of Evil
27 Nov.: UN weapons inspectors return to Iraq
19 Dec.: USA says Iraq is going against United Nations resolutions on disarmament

2003

2003 20 Mar.: War starts in Iraq with invasion by US and UK troops
9 Apr.: Baghdad is captured
13 Dec.: Saddam Hussein is captured

2004

2004 28 Jun.: Interim Government set up under Prime Minister Ayad Allawi

2005 30 Jan.: Iraq holds first free elections
6 Apr.: Interim Iraqi government elects first Kurdish president, Jalal Talabani

2005

Who's Who?

Abdullah Born in 1912, and murdered in 1958. Prince Abdullah was the Prince Regent of Iraq from 1939 to 1953, while his nephew King Faisal II was a minor. He then became Crown Prince from 1953 until his death in 1958. Abullah was a strong figure in Iraq and remained influential in government even after King Faisal II became king in 1953.

Aflaq, Michael Born in 1910, and died in 1989. Aflaq was a Syrian intellectual and teacher who founded the Ba'ath Party. He was a Christian who studied in Paris. Aflaq became a full-time political activist in 1942. He moved to Baghdad after the Ba'athist coup there in 1968.

Alexander the Great Lived from 356 BCE to 323 BCE. Alexander was a Macedonian King from northern Greece whose brilliant military successes enabled him to conquer neighbouring countries. His Empire eventually extended over much of what was then the known world, including Iraq. He ruled countries from Egypt to India, where he set up members of his circle as kings.

Allawi, Ayad Born in 1945. Allawi qualified as a doctor at Baghdad University and joined the Ba'ath Party. He left Iraq in 1971 and continued his medical career in the UK, where he specialized as a neurologist and then became a businessman. Allawi left the Ba'ath Party in 1975, and survived an assassination attempt in 1978. Dr Allawi was known to both UK and US intelligence as an Iraqi opposition leader. He returned to Iraq in 2003. Allawi was chosen as a member of the Interim Governing Council, and became prime minister of the Interim Government in May 2004. In the Iraqi elections of 30 January 2005, Allawi's party won only 40 of 275 seats. He remained as prime minister until Ibrahim Jaafari, leader of the Shi'ite United Iraqi Alliance, succeeded him on 28 April 2005.

al-Said, Nuri Born in 1888, and murdered in 1958. Nuri al-Said began his career as a soldier and became Iraq's chief of staff under King Faisal I. Al-Said became prime minister for the first time in 1930. He played a leading role in Iraq as a supporter of the monarchy. He was prime minister at the time of the military coup in 1958, when he was killed.

Arif, Abdel-Salam Born in 1920, and died in 1966. He was a career soldier who was president of Iraq from 1963 to 1966. He was killed in a helicopter accident, and was succeeded as president by his brother, Abdel Rahman Aref.

Bakr, Hassan Born in 1912, and died in 1982. President Bakr was a professional soldier who led the Ba'athist coup in Iraq in 1968. Saddam Hussein, who was a distant relative, was his security chief and became his right-hand man. Bakr resigned from his post in 1979 to allow Saddam Hussein to take over.

Bin Laden, Osama Born in 1957 into a rich Saudi family. Bin Laden's father made a large fortune as a civil engineer, constructing buildings in Saudi Arabia and elsewhere in the Middle East. Bin Laden came under the influence of Islamic extremists while he was a student and went to Afghanistan to fight the occupying Soviet forces in 1979. He became a leader of the Islamic extremist group opposed to all influence in the Middle East by the USA, and his organisation, known as Al-Qaeda, approved, funded and helped to plan the 11 September attacks on the USA. Following the overthrow of the Taliban regime in Afghanistan in 2001, bin Laden remained unfound.

Blair, Tony Born in 1953. Prime minister of the UK from 1997. Blair trained as a lawyer, and later joined the Labour Party. He was first elected as a member of the British parliament in 1983 and became prime minister in 1997. Blair sent UK troops to aid the US-led invasion of Iraq in 2003.

Bremer, Paul Born in 1941. Bremer is a career diplomat and former ambassador who became administrator of the Coalition Provisional Authority in Iraq in May 2003. He handed control over to the Interim Government in Iraq in June 2004.

Bush, George H. W. 41st President of the USA (1989–1993). Bush was born in 1924. He formed an alliance to drive Iraq's troops out of Kuwait in 1991.

Bush, George W. 43rd President of the USA (2001–due to leave office in 2009). Bush was born in 1946. He made the decision to invade Iraq in March 2003.

Cheney, Dick Born in 1941. Cheney has served under several Republican presidents in administrative posts and also made a success of his business career. He became a congressman in 1978, and then defence secretary under the first President Bush in 1989. He then became chairman and CEO of Halliburton Corporation in 1995. Cheney became Vice President of the USA in 2001.

Chirac, Jacques Born in 1932. After studying political science and administration, including a period at Harvard University, Chirac joined the staff of President Pompidou in 1962. He became a member of the National Assembly in 1967, as a member of a right-wing, conservative party. He served twice as prime minister and became president of France, after his third attempt, in 1995.

Clinton, William (Bill) 42nd President of the USA (1993–2001). Clinton was born in 1946. He launched an air attack on Iraq in 1998.

Faisal I Born in 1883, and died in 1933. King Faisal I was one of the sons of Hussein ibn Ali, the Sherif of Mecca, who led the Arab Revolt against the Turks in World War I. Faisal I became king of Iraq in 1921.

Faisal II Born in 1935, and murdered in 1958. King Faisal II was an infant when he became king of Iraq after his father, King Ghazi, died in 1939. His uncle Prince Abdullah ruled as regent until 1953, when King Faisal II reached the legal age to become king. He was murdered along with other members of the royal family and politicians in 1958 when a military coup overthrew the monarchy in Iraq.

Ghazi, King Born in 1912, he died in a car accident in 1939. Ghazi succeeded King Faisal I as King of Iraq.

Hammurabi Lived from around 1792 to 1750 BCE. Hammurabi was a Babylonian king who ruled Iraq. He issued an important legal code and ruled over a well-organized kingdom.

Hulagu Lived from 1217 to 1265 CE. Hulagu was the Mongol ruler Genghis Khan's grandson. Hulagu conquered western Asia and parts of the Middle East, including Iraq, ending the Abbasid Caliphate.

Hussein, Saddam Born in 1937. Saddam Hussein is the former president of Iraq. He rose to power through the Iraqi Ba'ath Party. He was responsible for Iraq's eight-year war with Iran from 1980 to 1988 and then for the Iraqi invasion of Kuwait in 1990. The USA and other Western countries suspected that he was not obeying the United Nations resolution telling him to get rid of his weapons of mass destruction. This led to the US-led invasion of Iraq in 2003. Hussein was captured by Coalition troops in December 2003.

Lawrence, T. E. ('Lawrence of Arabia') Born in 1888, died in 1935. Lawrence was an Oxford scholar and British army officer. He fought in the Middle East In World War I in the Arab Revolt against the Turks.

Mohammed Born in 570 CE, and died in 632 CE. In around 610 CE, the Prophet Mohammed claimed to receive the text of the Qur'an from the Angel Gabriel who appeared to him. Mohammed founded the Islamic faith and led a growing community of Muslims in the Middle East.

Nasser, Gamal Abdul President Nasser of Egypt was born in 1918 and died in 1970. As a young officer, he was the leader of the Egyptian Revolution in 1952. He became president of Egypt in 1954. He was much admired throughout the Arab world, including Iraq. He died of heart disease in 1970.

Putin, Vladimir Born in 1952. Putin studied law in Leningrad and worked in Soviet intelligence from 1975. Between 1985 and 1990, he worked in East Germany. He then worked in various political administrative positions in Russia, and became intelligence chief again under President Yeltsin in 1998. Yeltsin made Putin prime minister in 1999. Putin was elected president of Russia in 2000.

Qassem, Abdul Karim Born in 1914, and murdered in 1963. Qassem was a professional soldier who rose through the ranks and then led the military coup in Iraq in 1958. Egypt's President Nasser was his inspiration, but he was primarily an Iraqi nationalist who believed the country was being ruined by the monarchy and the politicians who surrounded the king. President Qassem was killed in the Ba'athist coup in 1963.

Rumsfeld, Donald Born in 1923. Rumsfeld became US Secretary of Defence in 2001. A former congressman, he has served in numerous posts in Republican administrations. He is regarded as part of the circle surrounding President George W. Bush who favoured the armed invasion of Iraq. He has also had a successful business career.

Schwarzkopf, General Norman Born in 1934. General Schwarzkopf was Allied commander in the Gulf War of 1990–1991. Schwarzkopf is a career soldier in the US Army who also served in Vietnam.

Find Out More

BOOKS FOR YOUNGER READERS

The Invasion of Kuwait, John King (Hodder Children's Books, 2003)
An account of Iraq's invasion of Kuwait in 1990 and the reaction to it around the world.

Iraq, Andrea C. Nakaya (Greenhaven Press, 2004)
A good source of information on the history of Iraq.

Weapons of Mass Destruction, James D. Torr (Greenhaven Press, 2004)
Looks at what weapons of mass destruction are and how can they be stopped.

BOOKS FOR OLDER READERS

A History of Iraq, Charles Tripp (Cambridge University Press, 2002)
An excellent general history of Iraq.

Iraq: The Bradt Travel Guide, Karen Dabrowska (Bradt Travel Guides, 2002)
A guide book to Iraq by an author who travelled to the country to explore the possibilities for tourism and who is a careful and fair observer.

Iraq: A Report from the Inside, Dilip Hiro (Granta Books, 2003)
Insights into the country from an expert author.

The Iraq War, John Keegan (Hutchinson, 2004)
A very informative book about the Gulf War of 2003, by a respected military historian.

ADDRESSES TO WRITE TO

If you want to find out more about Iraq, try contacting these organizations:

IN THE UK

The London Middle East Institute
Room 479
School of Oriental and African Studies
University of London
Russell Square
London WC1H OXG

The Royal Institute of International Affairs
Chatham House
10 St James's Square
London SW1Y 4LE

International Institute for Strategic Studies
Arundel House
13–15 Arundel Street
Temple Place
London WC2R 3DX

Council for Arab-British Understanding
1 Gough Square
London EC4A 3DE

IN AUSTRALIA

The Centre for Middle East and North African Studies
Macquarie University
Sydney 2109

The Centre for Middle Eastern and Central Asian Studies
Australian National University
Canberra ACT 0200

Index

Numbers in *italics* refer to captions to illustrations

A

Abbasid Dynasty 8, 9, 48
Abdullah 13, 52
Afghanistan 34, *35*
Aflaq, Michael 17, 52
Al-Qaeda 34
al-Said, Nuri 15, *15*, 16, 52
Alexander the Great 7, 52
Ali 8, 9
Allawi, Dr. Ayad 44, *44*, 45, 51, 52
Arabs,
   Ba'ath Party 17
   invaders 7, 8
   military coup 15
   revolt against Turks 12, 13
   support for Iraq 23
Arif, Abdel-Salam 17, 52
Axis of Evil 35, 51

B

Ba'ath Party 48
   Bakr regime 18
   members fired 45
   military coup 17, *17*, 51
   overthrow Qassem 16, 17
   resistance 38, 42
   Saddam Hussein 20
Babylon 7
Baghdad,
   air attack 38
   founding 9
   military parade *21*
   Mongols 10, *10*
   Ottoman Empire 11, *11*
   Qassem takes over 17
   revolt against British *12*
   war begins 4, *5*
Baghdad Pact 15, *15*, 51
Bakr, Hassan 17, 18, 19, 51, 52
   Saddam Hussein's closeness 20
Basra Province 11, *11*, 25

bin Laden, Osama 34, *35*, 52
Bitar, Salaheddin 17
Blair, Tony 36, 52
Bremer, Paul 4, *4*, 42, 52
Bush, George H. W. 25, 26, *26*, 52
Bush, George W. 34, 35, 36, *36*, 43, *44*, 51, 52
   declares end of war 4
   re-election 47
   threatens war 38

C

Cheney, Dick 34, 52
Chirac, Jacques 37, 53
Clinton, Bill 32, 33, 53
Coalition,
   drives Iraqis from Kuwait 26, 27
   takes Baghdad 38
Coalition Provisional Authority 42, 43, 44, 48

D

dictatorship 5, 18

E

Euphrates River 6, *6*, 8

F

Faisal I, King 13, *13*, 14, 51, 53
Faisal II, King 14, *14*, 51, 53

G

Ghazi, King 14, 51, 53
Great Britain, *see also UK* 19, 50
   control of Iraq 12, 13, 14
   Kuwait 25
Gulf War 31, 51

H

Hammurabi, King 7, 53
Hanging Gardens of Babylon 7
Hashemites 13
Hulagu 10, *10*, 53
Hussein, Saddam 53

attempts to murder Qassem 16
   Bakr's right-hand man 18
   becomes president 19, 20, 51
   capture 4, 51
   invades Kuwait 5, 24
   Kuwaiti oil 26
   loses US support 25
   numbers killed 33
   Oil-for-Food Programme 29
   palaces *29*
   Sunni Muslims 40
   suppresses Shi'ite uprising 27
   war with Iran 22, 23
   weapons inspectors 32, 33, 35

I

Interim Government 44, 46, 51
Iran-Iraq war 22–23, 51

K

Khomeini, Ayatollah *22*
kidnappings 43, 46, 47
Kurds 10, 11, 13, 49
   after the invasion 40, 41, *41*
   autonomy 30, 31
   chemical attack 22, 23, *23*, 51
   no-fly zones 30, *30*
   numbers killed 33
   rebellion 27
   resentment 19
   safe haven 51
Kuwait,
   invasion 5, 24, *24*, 25, 51
   liberation 27, 51
   Qassem 16
   UN Security Council resolutions 28
   US support 26

L

Lawrence, T. E. (Lawrence of Arabia) 13, *13*, 53

Index

M

Mesopotamia 6, 49
military coup 15, 51
Mohammed, Prophet 8, 53
Mongols 10, *10*, 11
Mosul Province 11, *11*, 13
Mu'awiya ibn Abi Sufyan 9

N

Nasser, Gamal Abdul 15, 53
no-fly zones 30, 31, *31*, 32, 51

O

oil 5, *5*
  discoveries 13
  future of Iraq 47
  Iran 22
  Iraq takes control of
    reserves 18
  Kirkuk installations *18*
  Kuwait invasion 24, 26, *27*
  Qassem 16, *16*
  rebuilding industry 46
  UN Security Council
    resolutions 28, 29
Oil-for-Food Programme 29,
  51
Operation Desert Fox 31, 32,
  33, 51
Operation Desert Storm 27
Ottoman Empire 11, 12, 13,
  25, 49

P

Persians 7, 8, 9, 11
Putin, Vladimir 37, 53

Q

Qassem, Abdul Karim 15, *16*,
  20, 51, 53

R

Revolutionary Command
  Council 20, 49
Rumsfeld, Donald 4, 53

S

Saddam *see* Hussein
sanctions 5, *28*, 29, 32, 49, 51
Schwarzkopf, Norman *26*, 27,
  53
Shi'ite Muslims 9, 49
  after the invasion 40, *40*, 41
  election *47*
  Iran 22
  Kurds 10
  no-fly zones 30
  numbers killed 33
  uprising 27
  violence stops 45
Soviet Union, support for Iraq
  16, 18, 19, 21
suicide bombings 43, *43*, 46
Sumer 6, *7*
Sunni Muslims 9, 49
  after the invasion 40
  British rule 14
  Kurds 10
  resistance 42, 45
  Saddam 22

T

Taliban 34, 49
Tigris River 6
Tikrit 4, 19, 51

U

UK, *see also Great Britain* 44,
  47, 49, 52
  control of Iraq 14, 15, 51
  future of Iraq 46
  Kuwait 26
  no-fly zones 30, 31
  protection for Kurds 27
  Qassem revolution 16
  reasons for war 4
  UN approval 36
Umayyad dynasty 8
United Nations (UN) 49
  George W. Bush 35
  mandate 47
  protection for Kurds 27

Saddam defies 5
Security Council
  resolutions 28, 29, 33, 36,
  37, 49
  US pressure 36
  weapons inspectors 32, *32*,
  33, 35, 38, 51
  WMD 4
USA,
  bombs Kuwaiti invaders 27
  Cold War 18
  future of Iraq 46
  Marines 5
  no-fly zones 30, 31, 51
  protection for Kurds 27
  reasons for war 4
  Saddam defies 5
  support for Iraq 23
  support for Kuwait 25, 26, 51
  UN approval 36
  War on Terror 34, 47

W

War on Terror 34, 47
weapons inspectors 32, *32*,
  33, 35, 38, 51
weapons of mass destruction
  (WMD) 4, 23, 49
  UN resolutions 4, 28
  weapons inspectors 32, 33
World Trade Center 34, *34*
World War I 12, 13, 25
World War II 14

Titles in *The Middle East* series include:

Hardback   1-844-43206-8

Hardback   1-844-43205-X

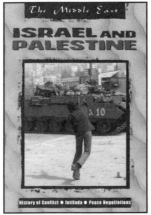

Hardback   1-844-43204-1

Hardback   1-844-43203-3

Hardback   1-844-43207-6

Find out about other titles from Raintree on our website www.raintreepublishers.co.uk